LIFE in the Future

CLONING AND GENETIC ENGINEERING

Holly Cefrey

HIGH
interest
books

Children's Press®
A Division of Scholastic Inc.
New York / Toronto / London / Auckland / Sydney
Mexico City / New Delhi / Hong Kong
Danbury, Connecticut

Book Design: Christopher Logan
Contributing Editor: Matthew Pitt

Photo Credits: Cover © Premium Stock/Corbis; p. 4 © Laura Dwight/Corbis;
pp. 7, 41 © Bill Varie/Corbis; p. 8 © Dr. Tony Brain/Science Photo Library/Photo
Researchers, Inc.; p. 10 © John Bavosi/Science Photo Library/Photo Researchers;
p. 11 © David Parker/Science Photo Library/Photo Researchers, Inc.;
p. 13 © Alfred Pasieka/Science Photo Library/Photo Researchers, Inc.;
p. 14 © Tom Myers/Photo Researchers, Inc.; p.16 © Hulton/Archive/Getty
Images; p. 18, 20 © Science Photo Library/Photo Researchers, Inc.;
p. 23, 25 © Reuters NewMedia Inc./Corbis; p. 26 © Quest/Photo Science
Library/Photo Researchers, Inc.; p. 28 © Chris Priest & Mark Clarke/Science
Photo Library/Photo Researchers, Inc.; p. 31 © Richard Hamilton Smith/Corbis;
p.34 © Joseph Sohm/ChromoSohm Inc./Corbis

Library of Congress Cataloging-in-Publication Data

Cefrey, Holly.
Cloning and genetic engineering / by Holly Cefrey.
    p. cm. -- (Life in the future)
Summary: Introduces cloning and genetic engineering, exploring the
technology and social issues involved and looking toward what the future
might bring as it becomes possible to duplicate even human DNA.
ISBN 0-516-23916-3 (lib. bdg.) -- ISBN 0-516-24006-4 (pbk.)
1. Cloning--Juvenile literature. 2. Genetic engineering--Juvenile
literature. [1. Cloning. 2. Genetic engineering. 3. Genetics.] I.
Title. II. Series.
QH442.2 .C445 2002
660.6'5--dc21

                                        2002001958

CONTENTS

Chances are you look in a mirror each and every day. Maybe you want to make sure your hair looks okay. Or perhaps you want to see how a new shirt fits you. You're not shocked when you see the reflection of your face and body in the mirror's glass.

Now, say you're walking down a street. You look up and see an exact copy of yourself. Only there's no mirror between you and your "twin." It's another person. You both have exactly the same physical features. Everything from the color of your eyes to the shape of your nose is identical. This time, you *are* shocked. With each passing day, this possible scenario becomes less shocking—and more likely.

Do you ever get a fantastic idea? Of course you do. And once you get that idea, you can't help but try to make it come true. Scientists get their share of bright ideas, too. They often have to be patient. It can take years, even decades, for technology and scientific knowledge to catch up with the imagination. Once it happens, though, the results are often well worth the wait.

Recent advances in science have led to two astounding technologies. The first of these is cloning. Cloning is the process of making an exact copy of another organism, or living thing. The second technology is genetic engineering. Genetic engineering allows scientists to make living things healthier than before. Farmers can grow bigger, juicier vegetables. Doctors can predict whether a baby will have a disease even before it's born! Genetic engineering even allows scientists to make new organisms.

When your parents were your age, there could not have been a book like the one you're reading now. Almost everything in this book would have been a fantasy back then. But now, cloning and genetic engineering are becoming a real part of modern—and future—life. In this

● *Genetic researchers hope to play a hand in ridding the world of its deadliest diseases.*

book, you'll learn how they work. You will see how these one-time fantasies have become the strange-but-true stuff of reality.

Each cell in your body performs a special role. Pictured here are red and white blood cells. Red blood cells contain hemoglobin, which allows them to carry oxygen. White blood cells aid the body's immune system.

CHAPTER ONE

Understanding the Terms

All living things are made of cells. The cell is a living, watery unit. It is the basic building block of all life. Certain organisms need only one block. Some bacteria and germs are made of only one cell. On the other hand, the complex human body is made of trillions of cells.

Cells perform many important jobs. They take in food and get rid of waste products. During the time they are alive, cells also reproduce, or make more cells.

⊙ TECH TALK

Though cells come in different sizes, all are extremely small. Hundreds of average-sized cells would fit inside the period at the end of this sentence.

BUILDING LIFE

Most cells have some common parts. They include:

• DNA (deoxyribonucleic acid) —a chemical substance that gives instructions to the cell

• Nucleus—a pouch inside the cell where the DNA is found

• Membrane—the cell's outer layer

To see cells, scientists must use powerful tools called scanning electron microscopes or transmission electron microscopes. Over the years, scientists have gazed through the lenses and learned much about cells. They've even learned how to alter cells. And by doing this, they can pull off some incredible feats!

● *Transmission electron microscopes, like the one pictured here, are nearly 400 times sharper than scanning electron microscopes.*

Since cells are alive—eating, getting rid of wastes, and reproducing—they need to know what to do during their life span. DNA bosses cells around. It sends messages to the cell about what to do. For example, when the cell gets the order to reproduce, it splits in half. Each new half inherits every aspect of the original cell, including its DNA. Each half—now two whole cells—then splits into half again. This process of multiplying by dividing continues until a large group of cells has been formed.

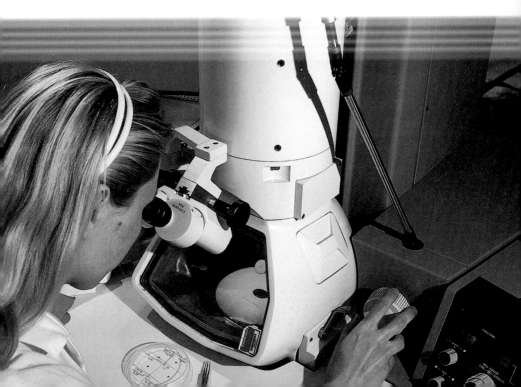

After a cell group forms, the DNA in each cell begins to assign more specific jobs. Each cell is told to change into a different type of cell. Soon the cells become blood, brain, or skin cells. Finally, once every role has been filled, a complex organism, such as a human, can be formed.

DNA also plays a role in what you look like. When viewed under a microscope, each strand of DNA looks somewhat like a twisted-up ladder. A specific set of DNA instructions is "included" with every human. The DNA is made up of many genes. Genes are responsible for our different traits, or characteristics. The genes we're born with are passed on to us from our biological parents. That's why you and your parents probably share similar traits, like eye or hair color. This process is called heredity.

DNA and genes are found in structures called chromosomes. Each human cell contains 46 chromosomes. Scientists have matched some of our traits with specific genes. In time, they hope

● *Within the twisted strands of DNA are 40,000 genes. Each one of them may have something to say in determining who you are.*

to learn the roles that each of our 40,000 genes performs.

By changing a cell's genes, scientists can urge the cell to grow in ways that it normally would not grow. By getting cells to grow differently, scientists can give an organism new traits—or even make brand-new organisms.

GENETIC ENGINEERING

Scientists who work with genes are called genetic engineers. Genetic engineers find an organism with desired traits. They locate the genes that are responsible for these traits. The genes are removed from the organism and then combined with genes from another organism. The second organism will develop the desired traits.

Suppose that you have two apples. One of them tastes delicious but is very small. The other one is gigantic but leaves a bitter taste in your mouth. You can eat a small, yummy apple, or a big, yucky apple. Genetic engineers would mix the genes to get the best traits of both apples. They would strive to make an apple that is big and tastes great.

Genetic engineering is also called Recombinant DNA Technology. Using this technology, scientists reshuffle and recombine the DNA from one organism with that of another. To do this, they use needles called microsyringes. Microsyringes implant substances into very tiny things. Scientists implant the DNA fragments of a desired trait into a cell. By doing this, genetic engineers can improve organisms. For example, genetic engineers have made tomatoes that taste better and stay fresh longer.

CLONING

Albert Einstein solved many of our scientific problems. Yet some tough problems could even stump Einstein. Have you heard the phrase "Two heads are better than one"? Imagine a room full of scientists who are all as brilliant as Einstein was. In fact, they all look like Einstein, too! If Einstein had been surrounded by people

The taste of vegetables, such as these tomatoes, have been improved through genetic engineering.

Many people believe that Albert Einstein had the most brilliant mind of his time. But if he had been cloned, he might have met his match—himself!

as smart as he was, he might have been able to solve even more problems.

This is the idea behind cloning. Scientists produce a picture-perfect copy of an organism. The clone possesses exactly the same genes as the original. Of course, scientists don't need to clone every kind of life form. They're concentrating on cloning only organisms that will help us learn more about our world and solve more of its problems.

Only Following Orders

To clone something, scientists take a cell and destroy its DNA—on purpose. Then, using a microsyringe, the scientists inject new DNA into the cell. The cell will now follow instructions from the new DNA. It's as if the cell is a soldier, simply looking to follow orders. The new DNA now provides those orders.

So when scientists want to clone an organism, they remove the cell's old "boss" (or DNA). Then they replace it with new DNA—the boss that the scientists want the cell to listen to. As the cell follows the instructions of this new DNA, it transforms into an exact copy of the original organism the new DNA came from.

Now you know the technical terms. But how did scientists find out about clones and cells, or genes and DNA? What discoveries were made years ago that led to the breakthroughs we're witnessing now?

Theodor Schwann successfully proved that all life was made from living cells.

CHAPTER TWO

Learning Through History

DISCOVERING CELLS

Cells were first seen under a microscope in 1665. English scientist Robert Hook examined a thin slice of cork in his microscope. He saw holes that were surrounded by walls. He used the word cell to describe these holes. Cell means chamber, or room, in the Latin language.

However, scientists didn't realize the importance of cells until many years later. In 1838, German botanist Matthias Schleiden said that he believed cells were the basic unit of life. In 1839, fellow German Theodor Schwann proved that all living things were made of cells.

From that point on, scientists focused their attention on the cell. Inventors began constructing more powerful microscopes. Scientists could now study cells more clearly. This clearer vision led to startling new discoveries. Scientists learned that cells divide. They also discovered smaller parts inside of cells, such as the nucleus.

DISCOVERING GENES

In the 1800s, a monk named Gregor Mendel experimented with plants. Mendel grew and studied thousands of pea plants. He learned that each plant's traits were passed down from parent to offspring. Mendel published his work in 1866. Scientists didn't pay attention to his work until the following century. But today, Mendel is considered a pioneer of genetics.

In the monastery garden where Gregor Mendel spent his life, he accomplished much. He conducted experiments in breeding pea plants that laid the groundwork of genetics. It took many years after his death before his work got the praise it deserved.

In 1902, Theodore Boveri and Walter Sutton discovered genes in separate experiments. Eight years later, American scientist Thomas Hunt Morgan discovered that genes are arranged in a special order. He made the argument that genes were responsible for heredity.

In the 1950s, the science of cloning began to take shape. Scientists Robert Briggs and Thomas King made clones of tadpoles. Amazed, other scientists tried their best to duplicate this cloning success. They tried to make copies of more complex animals, such as cows. These attempts failed. The technology and knowledge was still raw. The genes of these animals were too complex to clone at that time.

GENETIC ERA

Starting in the 1970s, advances in lasers and computers lent a hand to scientists. New microscopes kept providing clearer focus inside cells. The new instruments opened up a whole world of study. For the first time, genes and DNA could be observed in very close detail. Scientists also found ways to inject genes into many living things. Scientists made plants with new traits, such as a tomato plant that bugs wouldn't eat. Medicines were made by using organisms with altered genes. Scientists even injected human genes into mice. This created mice that were twice their normal size.

CLONING

Scientists need to have a lot of genes to perfect their work. Many genes get destroyed in failed experiments. In 1983, genetic engineers discovered how to make clones of genes. Being able to clone genes meant that researchers could have a limitless supply of genes with which to work.

Animals such as pigs, cattle, and rabbits were cloned in the 1990s. These animals were cloned while very young. It is easier to clone young animals than adults. The DNA in young animals is purer.

● *On March 5, 2000, the British company PPL Therapeutics announced to the world that they had successfully cloned healthy piglets.*

The animal hasn't lived long enough to have been affected by its environmental surroundings.

Attempts to clone older animals kept failing. Finally, in 1996, British scientist Ian Wilmut made a clone from the genes of an adult sheep. He named the clone Dolly. Dolly grew naturally inside of a female sheep. Dolly was born as a baby lamb, even though she was cloned from an adult sheep. Dolly's birth was a landmark event. It proved that basically any living thing at any age could be cloned.

Doctor Wilmut had tried his experiment many times until it worked. A total of 277 sheep either died or didn't grow correctly before he was successful. Since her birth, Dolly has been treated like a celebrity in the science world. Nearly every move she makes is monitored and captured on film. In 1998, Dolly gave birth to a healthy lamb. While Dolly possesses the same

● *In early 2002, it was revealed that the world-famous Dolly was suffering from arthritis. Many people in the science community are concerned about this development. They fear that the arthritis was caused by a genetic defect triggered by the cloning process.*

DNA as the sheep she was cloned from, her off-spring has its own individual DNA. Even better, the genes she passed to her baby did not cause problems.

A scanning electron microscope displays the image of a single breast cancer cell. Scientists hope that genetics will someday wipe out this disease completely.

CHAPTER THREE

Gene Genies and Clone Arrangers

Scientists are using their discoveries in creative, brilliant ways. They're striving to make our health, food, and bodies better than ever. They know that some genes can cause bad things to happen to us. Missing genes can cause hereditary diseases. Genes that didn't get copied correctly when the cell divided can also trigger health problems.

Some genes can get damaged if we fail to take care of our bodies. Chemicals, smoking, alcohol abuse, and too much sun can harm our genes. Damaged genes cause disease. Over 3,000 diseases have been traced to either damaged genes or heredity. These diseases include forms of cancer and heart disease. If damaged genes could be successfully replaced with genes from a healthy donor, many terrible diseases might be prevented in the future.

Making Medicine

When someone has diabetes, it means his or her body has trouble using and storing a sugar called glucose. The glucose builds in the person's bloodstream to dangerous levels. Diabetes develops when the gene responsible for making a substance called insulin fails to work. To stay healthy, people with diabetes must get frequent shots of insulin.

Now, thanks to genetics, scientists can help people with diabetes. They inject an insulin-making gene into harmless bacteria. The gene tells the bacteria to make insulin once it's injected into the human body.

Scientists have found over 500 genes that may be used to make medicines. One drug is given to children who aren't growing at the right rate. The drug helps correct the underdeveloped child's growth patterns.

Gene Therapy

In the 1990s, scientists hoped to improve human health by using genetic engineering. This branch of science became known as gene therapy. In gene therapy, missing or damaged genes are replaced with new genes. These new genes instruct the cells to make necessary repairs.

The future of gene therapy is filled with tremendous promise. Using gene therapy, some kinds of immune diseases have been treated.

Thanks to a genetic breakthrough, people with diabetes can get their needed insulin without receiving constant injections.

People with immune diseases aren't able to fight illnesses very well. They become sick easily. Scientists use gene therapy to help a patient's immune system get stronger.

Scientists are also trying to change the genes of damaged or dangerous cells. An example of a dangerous cell is a cancer cell. A cancer cell is a cell that grows out of control and endangers healthy cells. Scientists have figured out how to change the genes of a cancer cell. Scientists change the cancer cells so that they are easier to treat with medicines.

Gene Testing

Scientists have also created gene tests. Gene tests can be done on unborn babies. The tests will show if a baby will suffer from a hereditary disease. This allows doctors to begin treating the disease as soon as the baby is born. Gene tests are also given to children, teens, and adults. Genes can be taken from your blood, hair roots,

Were the crops shown here developed in the ground or the lab? With genetic engineering, people may not be able to tell the difference.

and cells in your mouth. These tests monitor a person's chances of getting certain diseases.

Engineered Food

Scientists make thousands of genetically-engineered plants. These plants have been used to make healthier, better-tasting foods. They've provided new medicines to heal the sick. Entire farm crops have also been engineered. These crops include cotton, corn, soybeans, and squash. The vegetables can resist disease and damage from insects and pesticides.

Scientists have also experimented with a plant that makes plastic! The scientists insert four genes from special plastic-producing bacteria into selected plants. Following their new orders, these plants soon yield a "crop" of plastic. Unlike the plastics we use now, this form is biodegradable. That means it won't harm our environment. Imagine— a plant that grows plastics bags.

Livestock are also engineered. Engineered dairy cows make larger amounts of healthier milk. The engineered cows that we eat have much less fat than non-engineered cows. Genetics could help to give us a healthier diet.

USES FOR CLONING

The main use of cloning is in research. Researchers try to find cures for diseases. They give cloned animals medicines and substances. Then they study how each animal reacts. These studies allow scientists to find out which things are harmful and which are not. They must use many test subjects to carry out these experiments. By using clones, researchers can perform many more experiments without running out of test subjects. They can make limitless copies of their subjects.

Plants are also cloned, often to conduct research on the environment. The plants are exposed to a wide array of chemicals. Scientists study how the plants react. This allows scientists to understand what is and what is not harmful to plant life.

Beyond the Lab

Have you ever wished that your favorite sports player could play every position at once? What if Sammy Sosa was cloned? He could swat a mammoth home run leading off a game. After his curtain call, the opposing pitcher would peer in at the next batter—who would also look like and be as strong as Sosa! Is this possible? Even if it were, is it a good idea? Would it be the right way to use this technology? Chapter 4 will take you beyond the lab. It will address human cloning—a subject with many questions but no easy answers.

People's concerns about cloning may soon be decided by political leaders.

CHAPTER FOUR

What the Future Holds

Cloning humans is a hot topic right now. Some people think human cloning is a great idea. Some wonder if the dangers are too great.

AGAINST THE TECHNOLOGIES

Many people are against human cloning. They include government and religious leaders, members of the public, and even some scientists. For them, cloning is too much like "playing God." Some believe that cloning could never be a natural way to create human beings. Others believe that human clones might be used improperly—perhaps as slaves or soldiers.

These beliefs have sparked great debate between those who are for human cloning and those against it. Cloning experiments are certainly not easy. Scientists had to clone a sheep nearly three hundred times before finding success with Dolly.

If a human were to be cloned, many attempts would also fail. Many babies would die before the first success story. Perhaps other babies would not be able to grow correctly. One thing is certain: Cloning is not a perfect science right now.

Some people argue against genetic engineering for similar reasons. They believe that it, too, is unnatural. They believe that we will change humans in ways that would be harmful. Others believe that scientists may accidentally create organisms that will harm us.

FOR THE TECHNOLOGIES

One strong argument for genetic engineering is that it repairs what we've done. There are many things humans do that damage our genes. We expose ourselves to dangerous, man-made chemicals and harmful rays from the sun. We've damaged our air, oceans, and ozone layer. It's natural for us to want to repair these things. Genetic engineering could help speed up the process.

Cloning could also repair what we've done to wildlife. Many animals may soon become extinct, disappearing from Earth forever. By cloning endangered animals, we could keep them from vanishing.

TECH TALK

According to the Union of Concerned Scientists, over 2,000 plants and animals have become extinct because of human actions.

ONCE, TWICE, THREE TIMES A BABY

Scientists are still trying to clone a human. But Mother Nature has already pulled it off. When a woman becomes pregnant with identical twins, the children have exactly the same DNA. That's right—identical twins are natural clones! In fact, they're probably closer copies than man-made clones would be. Identical twins are formed and begin growing in the same conditions—with the same mother to protect and nourish them. A clone, however, might begin forming inside of a different mother from the original child's mother. If that new mother had a different diet, sleep schedule, or exercise routine, it could slightly alter the clone's physical traits. However, the genetic makeup would remain the same.

Of course, one thing that can't be cloned is personality. You surely know this if you're friends with identical twins. Even if the two look identical, they certainly don't act and think the same!

Test Tube Babies?

Scientists in favor of human cloning want to use cloning to make babies. Some couples cannot have children. Some parents have genetic problems that they do not want to pass on to their children. If human cloning became a reality, childless couples could have children who are clones of one of the parents.

Legal experts believe that human clones would not, and could not, be mistreated.

A cloned human would have the same rights as any other human. If you were cloned, your clone would have your genes, but would be an individual. You may have your driver's license, but your clone would still have to take the test to get one. If your clone broke the law, you wouldn't have to go to jail.

Stem Cell Breakthrough

In November 2001, a company named Advanced Cell Technology Inc. (ACT) made a shocking announcement. ACT claimed that it had cloned a human embryo. Scientists, politicians, and the public were unsure how to mark this historic breakthrough. Was it something to applaud or to be feared? ACT workers insisted they were not trying to clone human beings. They said they were hoping to make important medical discoveries. They hoped to use the ball of six cells they produced as a source of stem cells. Stem cells can grow into any kind of cell in the body.

ACT believes that stem cells could help stop mankind's most damaging diseases in their tracks. They believe the cells could cure Parkinson's disease and diabetes in children. Stem cells might also be used to treat AIDS and cancer. In the future, some scientists believe that small pieces of skin could be grown into new hearts or brain tissue.

Still, there were many critics of the news. They felt that ACT's experiment was too close to human cloning. ACT admitted that their embryo could have grown into a human. However, it would have had to have been placed inside a woman's body for that to occur. At this point, American companies are not planning to cross that line.

IN THE WORKS

The future of genetic engineering and cloning depends on what we are capable of doing, and doing it safely.

● *The work of genetic engineers continues to open the door to many new, exciting discoveries about ourselves and our world.*

Scientists are conducting many experiments to see how far technology can take us. For example, engineers are trying to make small organisms that will help break down trash, poisons, and chemicals. If successful, this would make our environment a healthier place for all living things.

Scientists believe it's just a matter of time before they learn what each human gene does. This may allow scientists to one day wipe out all defects and diseases. It will also make cloning and genetic engineering safer and easier in the future.

biodegradable able to break down and be reabsorbed by the environment

cell the basic building block of life

chromosome the structure that contains genes and DNA

clone an organism that has the same genes as another organism

cloning using genes to make a copy of an organism

DNA (deoxyribonucleic acid) a chemical substance that gives instructions to cells

electron microscope a tool used to study extremely small objects, such as cells and genes

gene a section of DNA that passes traits from parent to child

gene testing tests to find damaged
or missing genes

gene therapy using genetic engineering to fight
or cure disease

genetic engineering also called recombinant
DNA technology; placing a section of DNA
from one organism into another

genetics the study of genes, DNA, and heredity

heredity the passing of traits from parent to child

membrane the outer part of the cell

nucleus a pouch inside the cell that contains DNA

trait a characteristic

FOR FURTHER READING

Balkwill, Frances R. *Amazing Schemes Within Your Genes*. Minneapolis, MN: Lerner Publishing Group, 1994.

Balkwill, Frances R. *Cells Are Us*. Minneapolis, MN: Lerner Publishing Group, 1994.

Jefferis, David. *Cloning: Frontiers of Genetic Engineering*. New York: Crabtree Publishing, 1999.

Marsh, Carole. *Cloning for Kids: Is One Enough, Are Two Too Many*. Peachtree City, GA: Gallopade Publishing Group, 1998.

Wekesser, Carol, ed. *Genetic Engineering: Opposing Viewpoints*. San Diego, CA: Greenhaven Press, 1995.

WEB SITES

Dolan DNA Learning Center: Youth Resources
http://vector.cshl.org/resources/resources.html

Family Village School: Just for Kids
This site has links to other Web sites about cells, health, disease, and nutrition.
http://familyvillage.wisc.edu/education/kids.html

Howard Hughes Medical Institute: Cool Science for Curious Kids
www.hhmi.org/coolscience

PBS: Genetic Testing
www.pbs.org/gene

ORGANIZATIONS

Dolan DNA Learning Center
Cold Spring Harbor Laboratory
1 Bungtown Road—334 Main Street
Cold Spring Harbor, New York 11724
http://vector.cshl.org

Genetic Science Learning Center
Eccles Institute of Human Genetics
15 N 2030 E, RM 2160
University of Utah
Salt Lake City, UT 84112
http://gslc.genetics.utah.edu

ABOUT THE AUTHOR

Holly Cefrey is a freelance writer. She is a member of the Authors Guild and the Society of Children's Book Writers and Illustrators.